Blueberries in Your Backyard: How to Grow America's Hottest Antioxidant Fruit for Food, Health, and Extra Money (25-page Booklet)

By R.J. Ruppenthal, Attorney/Professor/Garden Writer

1. Why Grow Blueberries? Six Great Reasons

2. Blueberries for Every Climate (and where to get them)

3. Grow Blueberries Almost Anywhere: Doorsteps, Patios, Balconies, Rooftops, and Yards

4. Perfect Blueberry Soil (regular garden soil kills them, but they will thrive in this!)

5. How to Plant and Grow Blueberries in Raised Beds and Containers

6. Feeding, Watering, and Caring for Your Blueberry Bushes

7. Making Extra Money Growing Blueberries

Chapter 1: Why Grow Blueberries? Six Great Reasons

Blueberries are delicious small fruits that cost *way* too much at the supermarket. These dark-colored berries sit near the top of the antioxidant charts. They contain healthful substances known to protect the heart system, fight cancer, lower cholesterol, and stabilize blood sugar levels. Clinical research has proven that blueberries can help keep skin and hair looking younger, while improving memory function as well.

A few weeks ago, the first local berries began to arrive in my local supermarkets, and now they're all over the place. I see them at the grocery stores, farmers markets, and fruit stands. With so many blueberries flooding the market at once, they should be cheap.

But just yesterday, I looked at the USDA's weekly report on food prices. Near the blueberry price information was a small note that caught my attention; "demand exceeds supply." As I write, the average national retail price for blueberries exceeds $11 per pound…just as my own "free" berries are ripening to blue in the backyard.

What if you could pick all the blueberries you want from your own backyard? Even if you have a small amount of backyard space in the city, you *can* grow blueberries, which perform very well in raised beds, large pots, tubs, other containers.

In fact, blueberries are one of the simplest plants to grow. In this booklet, you will learn how to grow them and enjoy a sweet harvest of ripe, nutritious blueberries. Blueberries have unique soil requirements (most garden soil will kill them), but they grow like weeds when you give them the right soil mix.

This booklet will teach you recipes for perfect blueberry soil that mimics the natural soil in their native habitats. Get the soil mix right and you are 90% of the way there. Blueberries are one of the easiest and most productive garden plants you can grow…perfect for lazy gardening.

Finally, you will learn how you can make some extra money by growing additional blueberries. Just a few plants can provide you with a productive harvest of these delicious berries, which are in high demand for their incredible antioxidant benefits. How would you like to enjoy an additional $720-$1200 per year just for growing these beautiful, worry-free plants in urban backyard space? With more space, you can make even more cash. All for only a few hours' worth of garden work per year.

Forget growing marijuana and fill your pot with blue gold. Blueberries are the new (and entirely legal) cash crop for home gardeners. You can earn a return on your small initial investment that will yield better returns than any business, stocks, bonds, derivatives, or other investment vehicles. Let's get started today!

Delicious

People love blueberries. In 2007, the average American adult ate 22 ounces of blueberries per year, almost double the amount people were eating ten years earlier. When blueberries are available, they are one of the most popular fruits around, which helps keep the price very high. Blueberry muffins, blueberry pies, blueberry pancakes, blueberry smoothies, blueberry jam, blueberries with yogurt, blueberries in your cereal...there are so many ways to enjoy them. People love that sweet burst of flavor and fruity aroma with just the right amount of tang.

Perhaps the best snack of all is just plain blueberries. We have several bushes in our backyard, and when it comes time to harvest, we give the kids some baskets to fill. However, most of the blueberries never make it into the house, since they are consumed on the spot. Any berries we can't eat within a few days are turned into jam or frozen for later use.

Blueberries freeze better than any other berries or small fruits. Individual berries do not stick together when frozen, so frozen berries are very easy to take out and use in any amount. Sealed up in a freezer container or double-zip locking bag, frozen berries will keep for up to a year in the freezer. If you can grow some extra berries, you'll be able to enjoy them all year long in cereal, pancakes, smoothies, and all your favorite baked goods. Frozen blueberries also make a great snack on a hot summer day!

Nutritious

Blueberries are nutritious additions to your diet. A one cup serving of blueberries packs plenty of dietary fiber, Vitamin C (almost 25% of your daily requirement), Vitamin E, Vitamin K, and manganese, plus smaller but important quantities of other minerals and B Vitamins. Blueberries have a low glycemic index with beneficial effects on blood sugar levels for people with diabetes. Plus, they are extremely high in antioxidants, as explained further in the next section.

Age-Defying, Skin-Protecting, Heart-Strengthening, Cancer-Fighting Antioxidant Power

Blueberries are one of nature's strongest sources of antioxidants. The dark blue, purplish color in their skin comes from pigment called anthocyanins, one of several healthful groups of antioxidants found in blueberries. Anthocyanins are powerful antioxidants which have been shown to have beneficial health effects in fighting cancer, heart disease, diabetes, and bacterial infections. Health expert Dr. Oz places blueberries in the #1 spot on his list of anti-cancer foods.

Research studies have demonstrated that blueberry consumption lowers overall cholesterol, protects the cardiovascular system, lowers and maintains blood pressure, helps regulate blood sugar, and improves memory function.

In recent years, blueberries have been studied for their anti-cancer benefits. A 2004 study from the University of Illinois tested the effects of blueberries on prostate and liver cancer cells.[1] This study's authors found that the antioxidants in blueberries help prevent cancer in all three of its stages: initiation, promotion, and proliferation. Researchers at Cornell University concluded that such antioxidants "are best acquired through whole food consumption, not from expensive dietary supplements." Translation: Don't take a pill; just eat your blueberries!

---

[1] http://www.imakenews.com/vitalchoiceseafood/e_article000402721.cfm?x=b4v1kpq,b2jwwny2,w

Most amazingly, the antioxidants in blueberries appear to be capable of slowing down the effects of aging by protecting human cells from damage. In a study reported on in the New York Times, elderly rats fed the human equivalent of ½ cup of blueberries per day showed improvements in balance, coordination, and memory. Other high-antioxidant foods (such as strawberries) also showed some improvements, but only blueberries showed such broad improvements. In another study involving elderly adults, participants who consumed blueberries every day for 12 weeks improved their scores on tests of memory and cognitive function.[2]

But the anti-aging benefits do not stop there. Blueberries also benefit your skin and hair. In 2011, *Fitness* magazine ranked "The Top Ten Superfoods for Gorgeous Skin and Hair", placing blueberries at the top of that list.[3] The antioxidants protect the DNA in skin and hair cells by neutralizing the free radicals which cause damage. Blueberries are an increasingly common ingredient in skin care products, especially for treatment of face peels and scars. The skin expert Dr. Nicholas Perricone recommends eating them[4] for skin care and longevity, including them in his recommended acne care diet. Celebrity nutritionist Isabel De Los Rios ranks blueberries #1 on her superfruits list as well.[5] Forget the imported and even more expensive acai berry; blueberries grown in the U.S.A. provide the best benefits.

In April 2012, the results of a huge study of over 16,000 women were published in a medical journal called the *Annals of Neurology*.[6] This Nurse's Health Study tracked the women's diets since 1980. The study's researchers also measured the mental function of any women over 70 who had not had a stroke. What did they find?

Those who ate the most blueberries and strawberries were able to remember things better than those who ate the least berries. The difference was equivalent to about 2.5 years of aging. One of the study's authors called it "compelling evidence" for the "memory benefits" of berries. While this study did not separate out blueberries from strawberries, one of the other studies mentioned above *did* separate them…and found that while strawberries helped achieve an increase on one of the three cognitive functions tested, only blueberries resulted in increased scores on all three function tests.

Expensive

Blueberries are not packaged by the pound; they are divided up into those tiny plastic clamshell containers. At the grocery store, they never show you the listed price of $11/pound or even $6/pound, which is about as cheap as blueberries get these days. Who is their right mind would pay $6/pound for fruit? You and I would; that's who. Once upon a time, these plastic containers

---

[2] http://www.nytimes.com/1999/09/21/health/blueberries-may-reduce-effects-of-aging.html

[3] http://www.healthguidance.org/entry/4654/1/Blueberry-As-Both-A-Superfood-And-Skin-Care-Treatment.html

[4] http://www.dailyperricone.com/2009/08/28-day-acne-program

[5] http://www.the5foodstonevereat.com/5-superfruits-you-should-be-eating/

[6] http://www.webmd.com/healthy-aging/news/20120426/berries-may-slow-memory-loss

came in a standard size of eight (8) ounces (one pint or half a pound). Nowadays, they have shrunk these clamshells to six (6) ounces or even four-point-four (4.4) ounces.

Out of season, people pay as much as $4.99 for a small container of blueberries, imported from some Southern Hemisphere republic where the sun still shines. This week, with blueberries coming into season in my area, my local chain grocer ran a special: $6 for two, six (6) ounce containers of blueberries. 2-for-1? What a deal; sign me up!

Unless you buy a larger quantity (such as one pound) at Wal-Mart, Costco, or a Farmer's Market, the retail prices on blueberries never get much cheaper than this anymore. So two containers for $6 sounds like a deal, but let's price that out. There are sixteen (16) ounces in a pound, so my two six (6) ounce clamshells total three quarters (3/4) of a pound. If three quarters (3/4) of a pound costs $6, then these blueberries are going for $8/pound.

Would you buy apples at $8/pound? How about peaches, bananas, oranges, or cherries? I get nervous when any other fruit reaches $2.99/pound. That is the price level which causes me to stop and think twice about how badly I want it.

Charging $8/pound is highway robbery, yet we are willing to pay that much for blueberries. The clamshell scheme is partly to blame for fooling us. But at some level we understand that we are getting a small amount for a big price.

There are several reasons for the high cost of blueberries. The first reason is soil: they cannot grow in normal garden soil, so you have to create a special "acidic soil" recipe for them. This is easy and cheap to do at home, but it is more difficult on a larger scale where these conditions do not naturally exist. The second reason is that blueberry bushes do not ripen their crop all at once. This makes it difficult for mechanical harvesters which pick everything at once, so even many large-scale farms have to hire real people to hand-pick the ripe berries.

The processes which can be automated run on the same energy that fuels your car, so when the gas prices go up, you can bet that blueberry prices will continue to skyrocket as well. Third, like other berries, blueberries are very fragile and have a limited shelf life. This drives up the cost of bringing them to market. Finally, because the fresh berries are only available in season and they are at the center of the antioxidant movement, they are in high demand.

Conventionally grown blueberries are covered with pesticides

Because blueberries are so fragile and have a short shelf life, they are kept "fresh" by spraying them with chemicals. No one wants to buy moldy or scrunched-up berries, but few people realize that blueberries are one of the twelve most contaminated fruits and vegetables in the United States. A recent analysis of showed that conventional blueberries are covered with as many as 18 different pesticides, fungicides, and other chemicals. Each year, an organization called the Environmental Working Group comes up with the "Dirty Dozen" and "Clean Fifteen" lists by analyzing pesticide data from the United States government.[7]

In a recent year, the government tested 726 samples of blueberries. While most berries came back clean, they found a total of 46 different pesticide residues on some of the berries.[8] Since you cannot test the berries for pesticides when you buy them, you are playing a game of Russian roulette.

You do not want to consume these pesticides and you certainly do not want to feed them to your kids. According to natural health and wellness expert Dr. Andrew Weil, pesticides are "associated with a host of very serious health problems in people, including neurological deficits, ADHD, endocrine system disruption and cancer. Whenever possible, avoid exposure to pesticides, including pesticide residues on food."[9]

Dr. Harvey Karp, pediatrician and author of *The Happiest Baby on the Block* added: "I really worry that pesticides on food are unhealthy for the tender, developing brains and bodies of young children... Studies show even small amounts of these chemicals add up and can impair a child's health when they're exposed during the early, critical stages of their development. When pesticide sprayers have to bundle up in astronaut-like suits for protection, it's clear parents want to feed their families food containing as little of these toxic chemicals as possible."[10]

The obvious way to avoid these pesticides is to buy organic blueberries. But buying organic is even more expensive. If you grow some of your own blueberries, you will have a lot less to buy. And perhaps you can grow enough extra berries to freeze for use throughout the year.

Easy to Grow

Blueberries grow like weeds in their native environment. Make them happy and they will thrive in your yard. Blueberries produce copious quantities of berries for very little effort. I have grown many different fruits and berries, mostly as a lazy gardener who does very little besides watering

---

[7] http://www.ewg.org/foodnews/summary/

[8] http://www.huffingtonpost.com/dr-walter-crinnion/organic-food-blueberries_b_594624.html

[9] http://www.ewg.org/foodnews/press

[10] http://www.ewg.org/foodnews/press

once in awhile and applying organic fertilizer once a year. Truly, blueberries are one of the most productive plants you can grow and they take very little time.

The only important trick with blueberries is to get the soil mixture right and feed them one additional ingredient to keep the pH low each year. I will explain how to do both of these below. After planting, your time investment will be almost very minimal…just let the plants grow and wait for your berries to come in.

Chapter 2: Blueberries for Every Climate (and where to get them)

Have you noticed that "local" blueberries have started appearing in the stores in places like Southern California and Florida? Originally, they could be grown only in colder climates because the plants require a certain number of winter chill hours before breaking dormancy in the spring. But these days, there are many varieties of blueberry plants to suit almost every climate. Chances are good that you can grow them too. Here is a picture of some homegrown berries:

Blueberries are a native plant found commonly in Northern states, Canadian provinces, and parts of Appalachia ("blueberry country"). The wild blueberry is the official state fruit in Maine, while the state of Michigan produces one-third of all blueberries sold in the United States. Blueberries are Canada's largest fruit crop.

If you live where it freezes for more than a few days per year, then you should be able to grow any kind of blueberry. They love cold winters, which encourage lots of fruiting, and the berries develop both sweet and subtle flavors as the cool spring temperatures warm into summer. Check with your local nursery or agricultural extension agent for some good regional recommendations.

Thanks to recent breakthroughs in blueberry breeding, even southern gardeners can grow blueberries too. Over the last few years, several varieties of Southern Highbush blueberries have been developed at university breeding programs. These varieties require very little winter chill and can be grown as far south as Florida and Southern California.

There are three main categories of blueberries: highbush, lowbush, and rabbiteye. Lowbush blueberries grow as a groundcover or a plant that reaches 1-3 feet tall. These varieties thrive in the coldest areas, including Eastern Canada, New England, and the Upper Midwest. Lowbush varieties are not ideal for a home gardener unless you have plenty of space. For greater productivity, most northern highbush blueberries (see below) can succeed in USDA zone 4 as well. If you live in zone 3, Hartmann's Plant Company has some "half high" recommendations such as Northsky and Northblue. (http://www.hartmannsplantcompany.com)

In the Mid-Atlantic States and on the West Coast, highbush blueberries are the best choice. These bushes typically reach mature heights of 5-6 feet, though some are capable of growing more than 10 feet tall. The first domesticated highbush blueberries were produced in 1916 in New Jersey by crossing lowbush blueberries with wild highbush varieties. Popular northern highbush blueberry varieties include Bluecrop, Elizabeth, Rubel, Duke, Jersey, and Legacy.

More recently, the subcategory of southern highbush berries has been created as low chill varieties have been developed for southern regions. If you live in a warmer region that does not receive much winter chill, check your local nursery or mail order sources for southern highbush varieties like Southmoon, Sharpblue, Misty, O'Neal, Jubilee, and the 3-4 foot dwarf Sunshine Blue.

A third category, the rabbiteye blueberry, is native to the southeastern United States from Texas to North Carolina to Florida. These bushes grow from 3-6 feet tall. Rabbiteyes have not had the same commercial success as other blueberries, but these are still the best-adapted berries for much of the Deep South. Widely grown varieties include Brightwell, Climax, Beckyblue, Powderblue, Tifblue, Chaucer, and Centurion.

Most local nurseries sell blueberry plants these days. If you want the dirt-cheapest prices, though much less selection, head to larger retailers like Home Depot and Lowe's. You will have a choice whether to buy small (1-2 year-old, up to one gallon pot size) plants or larger ready-to-fruit (3-4-year-old, perhaps 3-5 gallon pot size) plants.

Smaller plants are cheaper, usually $6-$15 or so. The larger plants can cost as much as $25-$35. If you are buying just a few plants, then the larger ones make sense, because they will start fruiting right away. But for larger plantings, the smaller ones are more economical. Blueberries can be planted from cuttings or bare root plants as well. If you are planting a lot of bushes at once, you might try to find some bare root plants or local cuttings to save some money.

If you decide to order your plants online, here are links to some reputable nurseries from different regions of the United States: Raintree Nursery in Washington (http://www.raintreenursery.com), Peaceful Valley Farm and Garden Supply in California (http://www.groworganic.com), Nourse Farms in Massachusetts (http://www.noursefarms.com), Dimeo Farms in New Jersey (http://www.dimeofarms.com), Stark Brothers in Missouri (http://www.starkbros.com), Bottoms Nursery in Georgia (http://bottomsnursery.com) and Hartmann's Plant Company in Michigan (http://www.hartmannsplantcompany.com).

In the United Kingdom, try Chris Bowers & Sons in Norfolk (http://www.chrisbowers.co.uk) or Ken Muir in Essex (http://www.kenmuir.co.uk). In Canada, try Cornhill Nurseries in New Brunswick (http://cornhillnursery.com) or Formosa Nursery in British Columbia (http://www.formosanursery.com). Some nurseries in the U.S. also will ship north of the border.

Chapter 3: Grow Blueberries Almost Anywhere

Don't think you have enough space to grow blueberries? Think again! They make terrific container-grown plants, producing large crops of berries when grown in pots that are filled with good blueberry soil. Grow blueberries in containers on your patio, doorstep, driveway, or anywhere else you can place a pot. And with beautiful foliage that turns from dark green to brilliant red (not to mention the white/pink flowers and then dark blue berries in season), these plants also make very ornamental additions to your landscape!

We have nine blueberry bushes in our yard, only three of which are planted in the ground (in a raised bed). The other six are growing in cheap plastic pots. Some of these are not even in the yard, but on a concrete patio. In the last apartment where we lived, we grew a blueberry bush in a pot on our second-floor doorstep!

Plants cannot grow as tall in containers as they do with more root space (unless you use really large containers, like wine barrels or tubs). But container grown plants can still be very, very productive. Our container-grown bushes are just as happy and produce just as much fruit for their size.

Don't believe me? Here is a picture of a TopHat Blueberry plant growing in a small container. These smaller blueberry varieties like TopHat and Northsky are no gimmick; they really can produce plenty of fruit. Let me give a shout-out to Gurney's Nursery, which sells these online. (http://gurneys.com)

Chapter 4: Perfect Blueberry Soil

When I give gardening talks, one common question people ask is "Why did my blueberry plant die?" Usually, they go on to tell me that their bush was growing well for a year or two and seemed healthy, but then it just...died. And the answer should be "Your blueberry died because you planted it in your garden soil." Most garden soil is too alkaline to grow blueberries, which thrive in acidic soil. If you give them the right soil, and make sure it drains well, then your blueberry bushes will reward you with many years of sweet berry harvests.

Acid Soil

Like azaleas, rhododendrons, camellias, and hollies, blueberries need to grow in acidic soil. Specifically, they need soil with a pH of 4.0-5.0, which is much more acidic than most garden soil. Acidic soil contains large amounts of organic matter, including peat moss, shredded bark, and pine needles.

Regular garden soil is slightly more alkaline, usually testing at around 5.5-6.5 on the pH scale. Unfortunately, blueberries are not able to adapt to higher pH soils, which prevent them from taking up the nutrients they need to grow. After about two years in the garden, the plants starve to death, even if the soil is rich in nutrients.

Instead, you need to create an acidic growing medium for them. And once or twice a year, you should check the pH of your soil to make sure it remains acidic. I will show you some easy ways to do this which will take no more than a few minutes per year. Once you put the plants in this acidic soil, they will grow like crazy and reward you year after year with lots of blueberries.

However, creating and maintaining acidic soil conditions in your garden is a big challenge. First, unless you have acidic soil already, you will need a large volume of material to make perfect blueberry soil. And you will need to monitor and maintain this acidity over time, since the pH conditions in your garden will moderate (becoming too alkaline for blueberries) over time.

Also, to accommodate the plants' roots, you will need to make the blueberry beds 12-18 inches deep with acidic soil. To make deep soil, you really have two options: build it downward or build it upward. Building it downward requires scooping out some of the old soil to a depth of 12-18 inches and heavily amending it (replacing most of it) with acidic planting medium.

This is a big job and there is a much easier way: build it upward with a raised bed. Or use some large containers to grow your blueberries, which is really similar to making a raised bed. Please see the separate chapter on Raised Beds and Containers, which I think are the best way to go for blueberries.

There are two blueberry soil recipes below. You will see they are widely different. This means that you have a lot of flexibility in terms of the planting mixture. But please make sure that peat moss, shredded bark, and/or pine needles make up more than 60% of your growing medium. This will keep the soil acidic and your blueberries should thrive in it.

What, you expected a blueberry muffin recipe? I think I said **blueberry soil** recipe! (By the way, check the Resources section at the end for a great website of blueberry recipes.) Here are two very different mixes I have used with good success. All materials are available at your local home improvement store or garden center:

1. Dave Wilson Nursery's Recipe (http://www.davewilson.com)
Use equal parts of these three ingredients: 1/3 pathway bark (1/4" pieces), 1/3 peat moss, and 1/3 forest-product-based potting soil.

2. Raintree Nursery's Recipe (http://www.raintreenursery.com)
80% shredded bark, 10% pumice, and 10% peat moss.

Well-draining soil

Blueberry plants also need soil that drains well. This means no standing water and no saturated soil underneath the surface. With too much water, their roots cannot breathe. While the same is true of most plants, blueberries are especially sensitive to this requirement.

The soil in your garden may not drain well if you have a lot of clay underneath. But if you have sandy soil, it should drain very well. Try this test: Dig a hole about 12 inches deep and 12 inches wide. Fill it to the top with water and let this drain. Then fill the hole a second time with water.

The second time you fill it, come back in one hour and measure the water level. If it has dropped by one inch in one hour, then your soil drains well. If more of the water is still there, then your soil is too heavy or compact to grow blueberries. If the water drains faster than one inch per hour, then it probably has a lot of sand in it. For a more precise analysis, you can get a soil test (just Google "soil test" online or ask your county's agricultural extension agent to refer you to a good lab in your region).

If your soil drains to quickly or too slowly, you can amend it. The best way to amend native soil is to add lots of organic matter, such as leaves, shredded paper, lawn clippings, untreated sawdust, or kitchen compost. Many of these materials take some time to decompose in the soil, though it is possible to plant in newly amended soil.

The much simpler route is to use containers or build a raised bed to grow blueberries. Then you will not have to worry about amending your native garden soil to the correct pH and drainage levels for blueberries.

My home is built on a thick vein of solid golden clay. When it rains heavily, the clay gets waterlogged and more water just sits there on top of it. Most vegetable roots cannot penetrate it. Even to build a vegetable garden, I first had to scoop out and remove as much of the clay as possible. I enriched the top few inches of the soil surface by adding in higher quality soil and lots of organic matter like compost.

After awhile, I just gave up and built raised beds. This turned out to be a great decision. My vegetable garden and my blueberries both thrive in raised beds or in containers on the patio.

Chapter 5: How to Plant and Grow Blueberries in Raised Beds and Containers

Raised beds and containers provide answers to all your problems. First, they allow you to control the soil inside. This makes it easier to keep the planting material acidic in the blueberries' preferred pH range.

Second, both of them can be made to drain well, so you can never drown your plants. Third, raised beds and containers can also keep the soil from compacting. Like most plants, blueberries love loose, deep growing soil for their roots.

There are many other benefits to growing plants in raised beds and containers. They bring the garden closer to our height, making life much easier for gardeners who are elderly, disabled, or have back problems. If birds start eating your blueberries, you can buy a few dollars' worth of plastic bird netting at your local nursery. Covering a raised bed or container is much simpler than covering a bush or tree that is planted in the ground. Also, raised beds and containers warm the soil more quickly so you get a slightly earlier start on your growing season.

Planting

Remember the potato chip ad slogan "Bet you can't eat just one"? You'll need more than one blueberry plant, too. In this case, it's not just because the berries are delicious.

Blueberry bushes need a second variety that blooms around the same time for pollination. Bees, bumblebees, and other flying insects with wings visit the flowers and distribute the pollen to other nearby bushes, ensuring a heavier fruit crop. So make sure you plant at least two bushes of different varieties. The two varieties should be related (e.g., both Northern Highbush types).

Plant blueberries in the spring as temperatures start to warm. Gently loosen and remove the plants form their nursery-grown containers, and place the plants in your soil at the same level they were in these small pots. Pack the soil around the plant roots just enough to keep the plant in place, but without compacting it too tightly.

Mulch them with a few cupfuls of compost or manure if you have some, or used coffee grounds if you don't. Water them in well. You can apply some fertilizer to the soil in a few weeks, but for now just let them settle in.

If you are planting bare root blueberries, you need to get them in the ground while the plants are still dormant. Put bare root plants in the ground as soon as the soil can be worked, late winter or early spring, before they wake up and start to grow leaves.

If your area is windy, and especially if you have highbush plants, you may want to stake them. Most nurseries sell 10-packs of the half-inch bamboo stakes or the one-inch wooden stakes, which are perfect for staking blueberries. Determine which direction your prevailing winds come from, and pound in the stake on that side of the blueberry bush, trying to keep it a few inches outside the current root zone.

Tie the bush to the stake using some orchard ribbon, twine, or trees ties (available at your nursery). Try to gather the main branches together in a loop and secure them firmly to the stake, while still leaving the plant room to grow. Staking helps support the plant and avoid too much stress from strong winds.

Here is a picture of some of my highbush blueberry plants growing in a raised bed. As you can see, there is a chicken run on another part of the same bed, separated by a portable fence. If you are interested in learning more about how to keep chickens in your backyard, please see my short book entitled *Backyard Chickens for Beginners: Getting the Best Chickens, Choosing Coops, Feeding and Care, and Beating City Chicken Laws*, which is available as an e-book and in print on Amazon.

Raised Beds

A raised bed is a place where the soil level is kept higher than the surrounding ground. Some people use the term "raised bed" to mean any bed with mounded-up soil. But for our purposes in this blueberry booklet, a "raised bed" also needs some walls to support the soil. It does not matter what materials you use to make a raised bed (it can be made of wood, stones, cinderblocks, or almost any material). Raised beds can be made in any size also.

Raised beds drain well because they are above the water level in the soil. Containers also drain well if they have drainage holes punched in them. If you have ever tried growing plants in pots that do not have holes, then you know all about losing plants to root rot and wet feet. Plants' roots need to breathe, but very few of them can breathe under water. It's one of those things they don't teach us in school.

The roots of blueberry bushes are fairly shallow for a large plant and do not have the extensive root hairs that some other plants have. A soil depth of 12-18 inches is all you need for them. A one-foot tall raised bed is just fine, or you can make it taller if you would like. You can leave it open at the bottom if you would like, so that plant roots can extend further down, or else you can line the bottom with plastic sheeting to create a barrier. Having such a sheet barrier may make it easier to maintain low acid conditions in the raised bed soil.

Of course, raised beds require more materials than traditional ground-based beds, so buying or building one is likely to require more time and money. At my home, I built seven 4x8 foot raised beds which are 24 inches tall. I used 2x8 foot redwood boards on each side, either 2x2 inch or 4x4 inch corner posts, landscape fabric for lining, and weather resistant screws.

Total material costs added up to around $500, which did not include the cost of filling up the beds. For this, I used many cubic yards of soil, compost, sand, and any organic material I could get my hands on, such as shredded cardboard, leaves, or hedge clippings. Labor was free, since I built them myself. I am not a skilled builder and these are not professional quality beds, but once I got the hang of it, I could finish one bed in a full working day.

That should give you some idea of the cost and labor involved in making raised beds, but you may be luckier than me. If you can salvage some building materials, you can save lots of money. Perhaps a home in your neighborhood is being remodeled and you can obtain some lumber or bricks for free. Maybe you have a good local source for stones, which could be set with concrete or mortar to make some attractive raised bed walls.

Or if you have a smaller space to fill than I did, the cost of building a small raised bed or two might not seem excessive. If this is the case, you might even consider buying a raised bed kit from an outfit like Gardeners Supply Company or Frame It All. In recent years, I have seen raised bed kits at Lowe's and Home Depot as well. I have no personal experience using these types of kits, but if they are well-made, then they might be a good option for some blueberry growers.

Containers

Containers make a great choice anywhere that it is impossible to put a full bed, such as on a doorstep, balcony, windowsill, or in a rented apartment where portability is more important than permanence. Of course, blueberry bushes may never reach their full size potential in a container (unless it is a very large one).

You can get a pretty impressive yield out of blueberries grown in containers, though. You can grow plenty of blueberries for your own use this way. If you want to make some money by selling extra blueberries, you probably should either go with raised beds or be prepared to spend a good deal of money on containers.

Choose a pot, container, box, tub, or barrel that is at least 14 inches wide. It can be made of plastic, resin, wood, clay, or metal. Generally, a 14 inch wide pot will support a similar soil depth, so that should fit within the 12-18 inch soil depth range that blueberries need. This is similar in size to a five-gallon paint bucket, which should work fine if you like the look. Make sure to clean out any used container and drill a few drainage holes at the bottom.

Blueberry plants grown in containers require one extra step to keep them growing and fruiting productively. You do not want them to become root-bound, which is when the roots grow around the inside of the pot so much they strangle the plant. You can avoid this by root-pruning the plants.

Every 3-4 years, while the plant is dormant in the wintertime (after the leaves fall off but before it starts to grow again), take the whole thing out of the container. Using a sharp utility knife, cut off the outer inch of the roots all around the outside and the bottom. Then put some new soil mix in the container (using the same recipe as before) and replant the bush again. This will keep plant in growth mode, but never outgrowing the container.

Chapter 7: Feeding, Watering, and Caring for Your Blueberry Bushes

Blueberries do not require much extra care. They are good plants for lazy gardeners. Give them acidic soil, regular water, and a small amount of organic fertilizer each year. Like any pets, they also appreciate an extra treat now and then, such as a mulch of pine needles or used coffee grounds.

Keeping the soil acidic

To make sure the soil stays acidic, you will need two things: a simple pH soil tester and some soil sulfur. Both are available at your local plant nursery. The pH tester is just a little gauge with some skewers on the end that stick into the soil to show you its acidity level. Try an online search for "ph soil tester" on Amazon or Google and you will see what these look like.

Soil sulfur is an organically-approved amendment which lowers pH. If you are growing just a few blueberry plants, a 4-5 pound box of soil sulfur should last for a couple of years. It can be sprinkled on top of the soil and watered in. Sulfur will not lower the pH immediately, but the pH will drop as it gets absorbed.

Blueberry Plant Food

Blueberries need the same three macro-nutrients as other plants: Nitrogen (N), Phosphorus/Phosphate (P), and Potassium/Potash (K). They also need other minerals in lesser amounts. While you can apply manure or good compost to the soil that supplies most nutrients, I strongly recommend buying a balanced organic fertilizer just to be sure. There are two good reasons for this.

First, to become a serious blueberry grower, you want to get the maximum fruit production from your plants. To get top production, you should not skimp on plant food. It only costs a few dollars anyway.

Second, you may be growing your blueberries in containers or in raised beds with plastic sheet barriers at ground level (which creates a big container). In either case, your plants will be entirely dependent on you for their nutrition, not being plugged into the ground. Therefore, you have an obligation to give them a balanced diet.

There are several different options for blueberry food. Cottonseed meal is available in most nurseries. It is made from seed husks which are a byproduct of making cotton and oil. Cottonseed meal helps support acidic conditions and its N-P-K analysis (about 6-2-2 or 7-3-2) is perfect for young, growing blueberry plants.

You also can use an acid plant fertilizer. This is the same kind used for Azaleas, rhododendrons, camellias, and hollies. Any nursery should sell it. Look for an organic brand of fertilizer, rather than one made from chemically synthesized ingredients.

Organic fertilizers contain whole ingredients which nourish the soil for long-term plant health. They also contain the trace minerals that blueberry plants need. Most organic fertilizers also supply beneficial humic acids and mycorrhizae fungi, which help the plants take up nutrients and stay healthy. Here are some widely available organic fertilizer options. Try to purchase locally, since the shipping charges cost more than the actual product when you order fertilizer online:

1. Dr. Earth Rhododendron, Azalea, and Camellia Food (N-P-K analysis of 4-5-4).

2. Down to Earth Acid Mix (4-3-6).

3. Espoma Holly-Tone (4-6-4).

4. You may have another good regionally-produced option as well. On the west coast, we have FoxFarm Happy Frog Acid Loving Plants Fertilizer (6-4-4).

Watering Your Plants

Water your blueberries once a week when there is no rain. Give them a nice deep soak, starting with perhaps 3-5 gallons of water per plant. You can increase this closer to 10 gallons for a large plant or if conditions are especially hot and dry. If you use a drip irrigation system, set it to provide about an inch of water each time. The water should penetrate the surface of the soil and filter down to the root level.

A slow watering is much better for plants than a quick one. A soaker hose, drip irrigation system, or sprinkler will dispense the water slowly enough that the soil can absorb it. On the other hand, the soil cannot absorb a lot of water all at once, which is why there is so much runoff if you empty a full bucket on the ground.

Speaking of buckets, one great idea is to convert an old bucket into a waterer. This works best with the five gallon paint or honey buckets (make sure to clean them out well first). Drill one hole in the bottom of the bucket, near the side. Place the bucket next to your plant with the hole covering the root zone.

Fill the bucket with water, which will drain out slowly. Go do something else for awhile, come back when it's empty, move the bucket to another plant, and repeat. If you use liquid fertilizers, such as fish emulsion or kelp extract, you can mix a bit into the water (following label directions) to provide nutrition for the plants. Bingo, your own homemade drip watering system!

For most of the year, water is the only thing your blueberry plants will need. You can cut down on their need for water by mulching heavily around the base of each plant. Some good mulch materials include untreated sawdust, used coffee grounds, straw, compost, and pine needles (or other conifer needles, like spruce, redwood, cypress, or whatever is native in your area).

By providing a thick mulch of at least 3-4 inches in depth, you will lock in a lot of the soil moisture. By itself, soil does not absorb as much water and it evaporates moisture into the air. This situation is better with blueberry soil because it is so high in organic matter already, but by mulching with more organic matter (such as any of the materials mentioned above), you will cut down on the evaporation.

Studies have shown that mulching can cut down on water use by 50-75%. Mulch also provides a thermal blanket for the plants' roots that moderates temperature levels. A good layer of mulch goes a long way towards preventing plant stress. It will keep your blueberries much happier and more productive.

Since blueberry bushes have shallow root systems, they can dry out without regular watering. This is a bigger danger for container grown berries, because the plants cannot take up water from the soil below. Check them frequently in hot or windy weather; containers can dry out very quickly.

Some home blueberry growers add vinegar to the water they use to irrigate their plants. However, experts disagree about whether vinegar raises or lowers the pH as it breaks down. Others put soluble sulfur in water to lower the pH. If you choose to do this, you will need to experiment with the proper levels.

If you have hard water (high in minerals), it may raise the pH a little. In addition, water with high amounts of certain minerals (such as boron or chlorides) can harm blueberry plants. On a small scale, this probably does not pose a big risk. But if you have decided to make a larger investment in blueberries (to make extra money), then get your hard water source tested to make sure it is usable on blueberries. If you are not sure, check with your local county agricultural extension agent.

Additional care

Once in awhile, you may see some brown sticks protruding from otherwise healthy plants. When these old twigs and branches are dried out (so you know for sure they are dead wood) go ahead and break them off. If blueberry plants have branches that grow together too densely, you are welcome to clip off any branches that compete with others. Just use some pruning shears or any kind of clippers. The plant will not mind being pruned. It is good to make sure that sunlight penetrates to all branches to promote healthy fruiting and ripening.

Blueberry plants are very hardy and are rarely attacked by pests or diseases. My blueberries have never suffered either one, and they are just about the only garden plant I've had which has not had some problem. The only attack I have ever suffered is from a few birds that steal berries in small numbers. You can solve this by netting the plants with the cheap plastic bird netting they sell at nurseries or putting out some of that foil bird scare tape they also sell.

In general, I think urban growers face fewer blueberry pests and diseases than some farms in the countryside. We are further away from wild stands of native berry bushes (which may harbor something that attacks a related plant species) and we have smaller gardens that escape the attention of many pests. If you find yourself facing a particular problem, have a look at this website, which is a very useful resource in listing and identifying blueberry pests and diseases (it has pictures, too): http://ipm.ncsu.edu/small_fruit/blueipm.html.

Harvest

This is the fun part. You get to pick the berries by hand. As your plants grow, you can bring a basket and fill it with berries. Pretty soon, you will need more baskets. If you grow a lot of blueberry plants, get some kids to help you pick them.

Blueberries do not all ripen at once on the bush. Each bush will have a few ripe handfuls one day and a few more the next. If you want to "automate" the process to harvest all at once, you can use a blueberry rake like the one sold by Raintree Nursery (www.raintreenursery.com). The downside of doing this is that you'll pick some unripe berries as well, lowering your overall yield.

Blueberries must be eaten or frozen within a few days. They do not have a long shelf life, especially if you pick them ripe (rather than half-ripe, like some of the ones in the stores). Freezing, jamming, and canning are great ways to preserve your berries for future health and enjoyment.

The U.S. Highbush Blueberry Council has a very nice, searchable website of blueberry recipes: http://www.blueberrycouncil.org/recipes.

Chapter 8: Making Extra Money Growing Blueberries

Blueberries are expensive to buy in stores (where, according to the USDA, "demand exceeds supply"). Growing some extra berries yourself is a great way to supplement your income. This section is designed to help break down the economics of growing blueberries, mostly in terms of helping you analyze the costs and benefits.

While these prices may change, they give you a good indication of what to expect. There are a few ideas in this section to help you start thinking about where to sell your extra blueberries also. Everyone wants homegrown berries, especially if they are pesticide free!

Anticipated Costs

1. **Blueberry plants**. One-gallon Highbush Blueberry, Lowe's, $9.98 (or three-pack of smaller plants for $12.99)

2. **Planting Medium**
   - **Peat Moss**. 2.2 cubic feet, Ace Hardware, $8.11
   - **Shredded Bark Mulch**. 2 cubic feet, Ace Hardware, $6.00
   - **Supersoil Premium Potting Soil**. 2 cubic feet, Home Depot, $6.97

3. **Raised bed construction materials**. If the bed is going to be 12 inches high, then it will need some walls. Try to salvage some wood, cinderblocks, stones, or other materials to use as raised bed walls. If you decide to use new materials, I provided some idea of the cost in the earlier chapter on "Growing Blueberries in Raised Beds and Containers". The cost can vary greatly, depending on the size of your beds and what materials you use.

Quantity of material needed: To fill raised beds that total 6 ft. x 9 ft. you will need 54 cubic feet of planting medium to fill 12-inch tall beds. (I am using this size as an example, because I will refer to it again in the last chapter.) Perhaps you have access to some leaves or compost for free, both of which are great additions. Extra native soil can be mixed in. You could throw in some shredded paper, sand, manure, or whatever other filler materials you can obtain.

These materials could constitute perhaps 20% of the overall total, but bark and peat need to make up the majority due to the acidic soil conditions needed by blueberries. Also, the more organic materials you add (such as leaves, shredded paper, or fresh compost), the more the soil level will drop over time as these decompose. So if you use more of these things, you will need to keep filling the beds, which is harder to keep doing after you plant the berries.

Another GREAT soil amendment for blueberries is pine needles (or needles from any of the coniferous trees, such as cedar, redwood, spruce, or cypress). If you have access to a bunch of this stuff (not only the fresh needles on top, but the rotting and decomposing needles underneath), then you can add conifer needles to your raised beds in almost any quantity.

But let's assume you cannot find any free stuff to use. Your local home improvement or garden store may sell bark mulch, peat, and potting soil materials at a cheaper price if you buy them in bulk (especially the bark mulch). Sometimes, you can get them delivered for free. But for sake of simplicity, and to keep our final calculation conservative, let's go with a high estimate on the cost.

Using the first recipe in the "Perfect Blueberry Soil" chapter for reference, we need equal parts of each of these three ingredients: peat moss, shredded bark, and potting soil. While the sizes are a little different above, let's just estimate that we'll need ten (10) 2-cubic feet bags of each at the prices listed above. This will be 60 cubic feet when we only need 54, but we're just estimating. This high cost estimate requires multiplying each bag price above by ten, adding the totals, and coming up with a cost of $211 to fill the beds.

How Much Extra Money Can You Make?

You may look at that number above and think: "There's no way I'm spending $200 on soil and filler." And I know I am not taking into account the possible cost of containers and of building raised beds, but I am hoping you can find a good deal on these or get some free material with which to make raised bed walls.

Whatever the initial cost, remember that this is an investment. Two mature highbush blueberry plants can fit in a 3 ft. x 6 ft. raised bed. An average-sized yard has room for at least three such beds with space in between for walking paths, which should still leave you enough space for your dog house, BBQ, or whatever else you have back there. That's a total growing area of 6 ft. x 9 ft., equaling 54 square feet.

You can grow two highbush blueberry plants in each bed, spacing each plant four feet apart from its bedmate to leave plenty of room to grow. Modern varieties of highbush blueberries are very productive, so you can expect a yield of 10-15 pounds of fruit per bush. Six mature highbush blueberry plants in 54 square feet can yield 60-90 pounds of berries per year.

Let's be conservative and take the lower figure of 60 pounds per year. I'll use $6/pound as a blueberry price, which might be a bit higher or lower than what you can get, but it's a low average at the moment that will give you a rough idea of the economics. With 60 pounds of berries, you could fill 160 of those 6-ounce clamshell containers. That's **$360 worth** of blueberries **per year**.

Can you find a little more space? Remember, you can build a raised bed anywhere, even on top of a concrete surface. One of my raised beds sits on top of a concrete patio, which does not matter at all because I built the soil upwards. The plants' roots have plenty of soil depth above the concrete.

If you're worried about toxins leeching up from the surface below, put down a few layers of plastic sheeting (available at your hardware store). Cover this with three inches of gravel at the bottom of your raised bed (and more plastic sheeting if you wish) before putting in your soil mix. Now there is no way your plants' roots can draw any substance from below that barrier.

In a bigger yard, you can easily double that growing space, with beds totaling 9 ft. x 12 ft. (or another similar combination) for an area of 108 square feet. That's twelve mature highbush blueberry plants producing 120 pounds of berries per year, filling 320 clamshell containers, and generating **an extra income of $720 per year**. This is a very low estimate, because these plants should produce 120-180 pounds per year.

Run out of yard space? Move that ugly old birdfeeder or take out the scraggly bush in the corner. I'll bet you can squeeze in a bit more!

Maybe your elderly neighbors next door are tired of cutting their lawn all the time (or paying someone else to do it). You could offer to put in a raised bed of blueberries and maintain it yourself. Blueberries are very ornamental plants all year long, a terrific landscape specimen. They have bright silvery green foliage in the early spring, gorgeous pink/white flowers that hang like little bells in the late spring, deep blue or purple berries by summer, and then the foliage turns coppery red or orange in the fall.

Offer me a raised bed of blueberries versus another useless green lawn that consumes too much water, fertilizer, and pesticides, plus needs to be mowed and maintained all the time with no real benefits…and I'll take the blueberries any day. I would even bet that the average blueberry bed probably requires **less overall work** and **less cost** in the space of a year than a manicured lawn. And just think of the rewards.

The neighbors agreed to let you build a raised bed on their yard? That's great! They are elderly and have heard about the health benefits of blueberries. The guy spent 20 minutes railing about the high price of berries in the stores. And milk prices. And gas prices ("back in my day, we used to pay 10 cents…"). So they were delighted when you offered to take the lawn off their hands and give them some berries at harvest time. Good people.

Now you've doubled your own 108 square feet and have control over 216 square feet. Try 24 mature highbush blueberry plants, yielding a low estimate of 240 pounds of blueberries per year, filling 640 clamshell containers. If we cut the neighbors in for 40 pounds or so (which is at least a year's worth to eat, jam, and freeze, plus give some to their grandkids), that still leaves us with **$1200 worth** of blueberries.

Can you use **$100 per month** in extra cash for very little work? That's enough to pay your cable or phone bill, bite a chunk out of your monthly food bill, put away a little extra cash, buy a plane ticket, or go on a cruise each year.

If you have access to more land (yours or somebody else's), you could get carried away with these numbers pretty easily. If you found a good sales outlet for a larger quantity of berries, then you could build a pretty good income just by farming the unused urban space on one city block.

Some neighbors are jerks and others are attached to their lawns, but a lot of other people either: (1) grew up on a farm or have some past family connection to agriculture, which holds nostalgic sentiment for them, or (2) are fully on board with the "local, organic food" bandwagon. Either type of person is likely to agree to your proposal and put their views into action, especially when they do not have to do anything for a promise of some free berries. So I think this scenario is not unrealistic at all.

And the estimates above are assuming a low conventional blueberry price of $6/pound, when in fact your blueberries will be local and chemical-free. People may pay more for these attributes.

If you are selling or bartering your extra berries, then you cannot label them "organic" without the proper certification. But you can promote them as "pesticide free" or "no-spray" which may get you a higher price. The vendors who do this at my local farmers market definitely sell more. And the independent grocers who label produce as "local" sell more of it, too.

Marketing Ideas

Farmers markets…hmmm. There's an idea. The ones near me (in an urban area) always need more vendors who are truly local, not "local" from 200 miles away. A few vendors are only there for a couple of weeks while they have produce in season, and then you do not see them again for awhile. Other possible sales outlets include fruit stands and neighborhood grocery stores. Many independent grocers will buy produce from local farmers in season.

In my area, there is someone who grows raspberries in his backyard. They are all purchased by a very expensive local restaurant, which makes them into desserts in season. School cafeterias, local social clubs, and "lemonade stands" on the street corner are just a few other suggestions.

And while you may not be keen on selling to your friends and neighbors (though I wouldn't hold it against you), what about bartering? If the woman down the street raises chickens and has extra eggs, maybe you can strike a bargain for some of your blueberries. If a family up the hill has a nut tree, maybe they will let you gather all you want if you offer them some goodwill berries.

Predicting the Future

Unless you start out with larger plants, it will take 5-6 years for your blueberry plants to mature (though you can expect a few handfuls of berries by the second year and growing quantities thereafter). Your payoff is not immediate, but it is one heck of an investment. Once your plants begin to produce a full load in 5-6 years, you will be doubling your initial investment every year. Happy blueberry bushes can live as long as 60 years. They may still be there for the next generation to enjoy.

Since this is a medium-term business opportunity (five years in the future), it makes sense to ask one more question: what is the outlook for blueberry prices? The outlook is this: sky-high prices and the availability of new cultivars for southern climates has encouraged farmers to plant more acres of blueberries. Supply is growing, so the price may come down a little.

But balance that with the news that blueberry consumption doubled over the last ten year period that was studied. And that ten year period (through 2007) did not include most of the new research into blueberries' health benefits. With the U.S. government reporting that "demand exceeds supply", I think the next round of numbers on consumption will show that blueberry demand is skyrocketing well beyond these previous figures. How else can they charge $8-11 per pound for something?

Consider this also: the U.S. population (like that of many other countries) is rapidly aging. Baby boomers are just starting to retire, and this is the largest demographic group that has ever moved into old age at once. This is the same segment of the market which has solidly embraced the movement toward more natural health remedies.

If you produced a drug that helped people retain some youth in their skin, hair, and memory, you would see a very bright future for that product over the next few years. Here, you have just that product, but it does not require FDA approval. Every type of fruit and vegetable has been studied for its antioxidant benefits and blueberries routinely come out on top; that fact will not change.

Demographically, a population the size of Pennsylvania is expected to retire in Florida alone in the next few years. As more northerners (with a taste for blueberries) retire in southern climates, they also will help spread the taste for berries to markets that are not accustomed to consuming as much. Supply may grow, but demand is growing rapidly, also (maybe more rapidly than supply).

For all these reasons and many more, there will be plenty of blueberry demand for years to come. Even if the price falls a bit with added supply, it cannot fall too much, because blueberries are just too expensive for commercial farms to grow, harvest, and ship. Nature has dictated that blueberries will continue to be a high-priced commodity.

Show me any business, stock, bond, derivative, or investment vehicle with such a high probability of success and so little risk. Show me any other business or investment with a substantial likelihood of doubling your investment in five years. And doubling it again the next year. And the year after that, continuing for years, and even decades into the future.

Money really does grow on trees (or, in this case, bushes).

Show me a more wholesome way to make a few extra bucks than providing people with a delicious, nutritious, and healthy snack like blueberries. This is a good thing to do. If you decide this is a worthwhile venture, then wish you the best of success in your pursuit of blue gold.

Conclusion

I cannot promise you 100% success with blueberries. Some unforeseen issue may occur along the way. But blueberries are very strong, adaptable plants which grow like weeds in the wild. Even "black thumb" gardeners have found them very forgiving in the home garden. Given their great taste, powerful antioxidant benefits for health, and expensive cost in the supermarket, it makes sense to consider growing blueberries in your home garden. And as long as blueberries remain so popular for food and health, you may be able to make some extra money at the same time.

Resources

Blueberry Recipes: Muffins, pancakes, shakes, salads, desserts, and much more, from the U.S. Highbush Blueberry Council, http://www.blueberrycouncil.org/recipes.

Blueberry Nutrition: The WH Foods site has a thorough profile, http://www.whfoods.com/genpage.php?tname=nutrientprofile&dbid=84.

Which Fruits and Veggies are Most Toxic? EWG's Dirty Dozen, http://www.ewg.org/foodnews/summary.

Blueberry Pests and Diseases: http://ipm.ncsu.edu/small_fruit/blueipm.html.

More Info on Growing Blueberries:

    1. Dave Wilson Nursery, Growing Blueberries in Containers. http://www.davewilson.com/homegrown/promotion/bluecontainer.html

    2. University of Florida IFAS Extension. http://edis.ifas.ufl.edu/mg359

    3. University of Kentucky Cooperative Extension. http://www.ca.uky.edu/agc/pubs/ho/ho60/ho60.htm

4. University of Minnesota Extension.
http://www.extension.umn.edu/distribution/horticulture/dg3463.html

5. University of New Hampshire Extension.
http://extension.unh.edu/resources/representation/Resource000578_Rep600.pdf

6. Oregon State University Extension Service.
http://extension.oregonstate.edu/gardening/node/1013

7. North Carolina State University, Cooperative Extension Service.
http://www.ces.ncsu.edu/depts/hort/hil/hil-8207.html

Longer Books with More In-Depth Information:

1. *The Backyard Berry Book: A Hands-On Guide to Growing Berries, Brambles, and Vine Fruit in the Home Garden* by Stella Otto (Ottographics 1995).
http://www.amazon.com/The-Backyard-Berry-Book-Hands-On/dp/0963452061/ref=sr_1_1?ie=UTF8&qid=1337887045&sr=8-1

2. *Fruits and Berries for the Home Garden* by Lewis Hill (Storey Publishing 1992).
http://www.amazon.com/Fruits-Berries-Home-Garden-Lewis/dp/0882667637/ref=sr_1_3?ie=UTF8&qid=1337887045&sr=8-3

3. *The Berry Grower's Companion* by Barbara Bowling (Timber Press 2005).
http://www.amazon.com/Berry-Growers-Companion-Barbara-Bowling/dp/0881927260/ref=sr_1_4?ie=UTF8&qid=1337887045&sr=8-4

My Other Publications, all available at www.amazon.com
(Click my author name on Amazon to see up to date titles)

1. Backyard Chickens for Beginners: Getting the Best Chickens, Choosing Coops, Feeding and Care, and Beating City Chicken Laws

Description from Amazon:
Excellent booklet for beginners on how to start a backyard mini-flock of 2-4 chickens and get fresh eggs every day. Written by the author of the best-selling Fresh Food From Small Spaces book, a former columnist for Urban Farm magazine. (Updated 2012 Version)

Topics include:
• Fresh Eggs Every Day
• How Much Space Do You Need?
• Building or Buying a Coop
• Feeders, Waterers, Nesting Boxes, and Roosts
• Getting Chicks or Chickens
• Feeding Your Chickens
• Tips for Cold Climates

• Health and Safety
• Dealing with Neighbors, City Chicken Laws, and Other Challenges
• Resources: Everything You Need!

2. How to Grow Potatoes: Planting and Harvesting Organic Food From Your Patio, Rooftop, Balcony, or Backyard Garden

Perfect beginners guide to growing potatoes. This booklet explains how to plant and grow organic potatoes for food in the home garden. Recommended for backyard gardeners and container gardeners with small city-sized yards, patios, balconies, decks, and rooftops.

• Why Grow Potatoes? Six Great Reasons
• Different Kinds of Potatoes (and Where to Get Them)
• Growing in Containers, Raised Beds, and Traditional Rows
• Planting and Hilling Potatoes
• Soil, Fertilizer, and Watering Needs
• Harvesting Potatoes
• Storing Potatoes for Later Use
• *Bonus*: Two Secret Tips for Getting More (and More Delicious) Potatoes

3. Fall and Winter Gardening: 25 Organic Vegetables to Plant and Grow for Late Season Food

Description from Amazon:
Complete guide to growing organic vegetables for a fall and winter garden. This book explains which vegetables can survive in cold weather and how to grow them. Recommended for backyard gardeners and container gardeners who want to grow food for fresh eating all year round.

Topics Include

• Introduction to Late Season Vegetable Gardening
• 25 Vegetables for Cool Seasons
• Starting Vegetables From Seed
• When to Plant in Your Area
• Preparing the Soil and Fertilizing
• Garden Rows, Raised Beds, and Containers
• Extending Your Season
• Harvesting and Storing Your Produce
• Resources: More Information

4. Fresh Food From Small Spaces: The Square-Inch Gardener's Guide to Year-Round Growing, Fermenting, and Sprouting, by R.J. Ruppenthal (Chelsea Green Publishing 2008).
This book covers small space gardening, fermenting (yogurt, kefir, sauerkraut, and kimchi), sprouting, plus chickens for eggs and bees for honey. Over 20,000 people have read this book, which helps beginners learn what they can grow in small urban spaces, such as apartments,

condominiums, townhouses, and small homes. Many readers have been motivated to try new things and grow some food where they did not believe they could before reading this. The book is a broad overview, so it does not have a fine level of detail.

Author Info

R.J. Ruppenthal is a licensed attorney and college professor in California who has a passion for growing and raising some of his own food. He regularly writes and blogs about fruit and vegetable gardening, growing food in small urban spaces, sustainability, and raising backyard chickens. On occasion, he even puts his degrees to use and writes something about law or government. You can follow his blogs at http://backyardcvf.blogspot.com or on his Amazon Author's Page here: http://www.amazon.com/R.J.-Ruppenthal/e/B00852ZTT2/ref=ntt_athr_dp_pel_1.

Made in the USA
Middletown, DE
17 June 2018